PROPHETIC BOOTCAMP

SIMPLE GUIDELINES AND ACTIVATIONS
TO LIVE A PROPHETIC LIFESTYLE

PROPHETIC BOOTCAMP

SIMPLE GUIDELINES AND ACTIVATIONS
TO LIVE A PROPHETIC LIFESTYLE

KAWIKA CORNELIUS
FOREWORD BY JOAN HUNTER

PROPHETIC BOOTCAMP
SIMPLE GUIDELINES AND ACTIVATIONS TO LIVE A PROPHETIC LIFESTYLE
KAWIKA CORNELIUS

Copyright © 2025 Kawika Cornelius. All rights reserved. Except for brief quotations for review purposes, no part of this book may be reproduced in any form without prior written permission from the author.

Unless otherwise marked, all scriptures are taken from the NEW KING JAMES VERSION (NKJV): Scripture taken from the NEW KING JAMES VERSION®. Copyright© 1982 by Thomas Nelson, Inc. Used by permission. All rights reserved.

Scriptures marked NAS are taken from the NEW AMERICAN STANDARD (NAS): Scripture taken from the NEW AMERICAN STANDARD BIBLE®, copyright© 1960, 1962, 1963, 1968, 1971, 1972, 1973, 1975, 1977, 1995 by The Lockman Foundation. Used by permission.

Scriptures marked NIV are taken from the NEW INTERNATIONAL VERSION (NIV): Scripture taken from THE HOLY BIBLE, NEW INTERNATIONAL VERSION ®. Copyright© 1973, 1978, 1984, 2011 by Biblica, Inc.™. Used by permission of Zondervan.

Published by:
LIFEWISE BOOKS
PO BOX 1072
Pinehurst, TX 77362
LifeWiseBooks.com

To contact the author: www.freedomandjoycc.org

Print - 978-1-958820-99-5
Ebook - 978-1-969827-00-6

DEDICATION

I want to dedicate this mini-equipping book to Dr. Joelle Suel, a spiritual mother and prophetic voice in my life who highlighted, prophesied, and activated my prophetic calling in 2004. Her investment in my life is making history.

Thank you, Dr. Joelle, for launching me forward into my God-given destiny. This book is the fruit of that!

CONTENTS

Foreword ix

Introduction 1

CHAPTER 1
What is the Prophetic? 3

CHAPTER 2
How Does God Speak? 9

CHAPTER 3
Prophetic Guidelines 15

CHAPTER 4
Let's Prophesy! 21

CHAPTER 5
Testing the Voice 27

CHAPTER 6
Steward Your Word 31

CHAPTER 7
Prophetic Evangelism   35

CHAPTER 8
Aligned with Oil   39

CONCLUSION
Learn It, Own It, Multiply!   43

About the Author   45

Endnotes   47

FOREWORD

Prophetic Bootcamp is a timely and powerful introduction to the ministry of prophecy, while also highlighting the lifestyle that sustains and promotes effective prophetic ministry. In this book, Kawika Cornelius has provided a clear, practical, and Spirit-led manual on one of the most vital ministries for the body of Christ. It will be of great benefit to every believer who desires to grow in hearing and releasing the voice of God.

Prophecy is the act of revealing the heart of God to a person, a people, or a nation so that His glory is revealed, His purposes are fulfilled, and mankind is delivered from evil. It is the supernatural means by which God draws His people into His throne room, directing their paths and empowering them to overcome the world, the flesh, and the devil.

When done rightly, prophecy is nothing less than the manifestation of Jesus Himself in a given moment. It is the unveiling of His love, His wisdom, and His patient leading of His sheep. This is why it is essential for the church to learn how to release His word with accuracy and integrity—in season and out of season, both within the walls of the church and in the highways and byways of everyday life.

As you read and meditate on the truths within this book, I encourage you to commit yourself to becoming a vessel of His voice. The world is longing for an encounter with authentic Christianity, and there is no clearer expression of that than when God's people faithfully release His heart through prophecy.

JOAN HUNTER
Evangelist / Author
Host of *Miracles Happen!* TV show

INTRODUCTION

When was the last time you heard the voice of God for yourself? Did you know that God invites you to hear Him daily? Often, I hear believers ask me, "Can you hear God for me? Because I can't hear Him for myself." The goal of this book is to make hearing God's voice easy and accessible for every reader. Jesus wants you to be His mouthpiece to the world!

My prayer is that as you read through this book, you are stirred, equipped, and activated to hear the voice of God personally every day. There's nothing better than living a life led by Him. I believe that these truths become a doorway for you to encounter Jesus, and be an encounter with Him everywhere you go. Buckle up and get ready to learn; it's time to prophesy.

CHAPTER 1
WHAT IS THE PROPHETIC?

The prophetic can be summed up into four gifts of the Spirit: the gift of prophecy, the gift of the word of knowledge, the gift of discerning of spirits, and the gift of the word of wisdom. as you learn how these gifts operate, as God wills, you'll find that they all work together to communicate God's heart to an individual.

What exactly are the Gifts of the Spirit? Gifts of the Spirit are special abilities provided by the Holy Spirit to Christians for the purpose of building up the Body of Christ and reaching those who don't know Jesus.

1 Corinthians 12:7-11 lists the nine spiritual gifts:

"But the manifestation of the Spirit is given to each one for the profit of all: for to one is given the word of wisdom through the Spirit, to another the word of knowledge through the same Spirit, to another faith by the same Spirit, to another gifts of healings by the same Spirit, to another the working of miracles, to another prophecy, to another discerning of spirits, to another different kinds of tongues, to another the interpretation of tongues. But one and the same Spirit works all these things, distributing to each one individually as He wills."

Spiritual gifts are given by the Holy Spirit to edify and build people up. In 1 Corinthians 14:12 (NAS), Paul exhorts us, saying, "Since you are eager to possess spiritual gifts, strive to excel for the edification of the church." This training is to equip you to build people up!

> *Hearing God's voice personally is the everyday privilege of every believer.*
>
> "My sheep hear My voice, and I know them, and they follow Me." John 10:27

Let's get excited to grow in the prophetic!

GOD CALLS YOU TO PROPHESY!

When I was younger, I always looked up to those who prophesied, never imagining I would ever be graced to operate and function in the prophetic like them. This mindset was a lie from the pit of hell! We are all invited and encouraged to prophesy.

> *Every believer is told to
> especially desire to prophesy!*
>
> "Pursue love, and desire spiritual gifts, but
> especially that you may prophesy."
> 1 Corinthians 14:1

> *Every believer can learn to prophesy
> and to encourage all.*
>
> "For you can all prophesy one by one, that all
> may learn and all may be encouraged."
> 1 Corinthians 14:31

The Gift of Discerning of Spirits

The supernatural ability to discern the move of the Holy Spirit, angelic spirits, demonic spirits, and the human spirit. This gift enables you to see where the Lord is operating, where to encourage partnership, and where the enemy is operating, so you can remove his operation.

The Gift of the Word of Wisdom

The ability to discern and declare the proper wisdom for a person or situation. This gift is also very helpful in providing wisdom on how to communicate what you discern in the spiritual realm, words of knowledge, and prophecy. The words we deliver must always go through the filter of edification so that what we say builds people up (1 Corinthians 14:12).

As you grow in operating in the prophetic gifts, you'll see the four gifts listed above often overlapping and working together to communicate supernatural encouragement to others.

SIMPLE DEFINITIONS

The Gift of Prophecy

Hebrew definition:

- "To flow forth or bubble up with inspiration."[1]
- "To speak for another."[2]

Greek definition:

- "To predict."[3]
- "To speak forth the mind and counsel of God."[4]

Larry Randolph (author and pastor known for his prophetic voice) defines it as:

- "God sharing secrets with his friends."[5]

This gift enables you to edify, comfort, and encourage people, as the Lord's mouthpiece.

The Gift of the Word of Knowledge

The ability to discern and declare things known to others but unknown to you at the time. This gift enables you to see details about a person so you know how to build them up.

CHAPTER 2
HOW DOES GOD SPEAK?

How does God communicate prophecy, words of knowledge and wisdom, and the discerning of spirits to us? Biblically, there are many ways. Here are some of the most common ways God speaks to us:

His Still Small Voice

As he waited to hear the Lord's voice in 1 Kings 19:11-13, Elijah heard a strong wind, felt an earthquake, and saw fire, but the Lord wasn't in them. Finally, Elijah heard the Lord's still small voice. God's still-small inner voice is a common, everyday occurrence for believers.

Visions

An internal vision is simply a picture or movie reel you see in your imagination. An external vision is a picture or movie reel that you literally see outside of you. It's when the realm of the Spirit becomes more tangible and seen than your natural surroundings. God speaks both ways. Visions are a common, everyday occurrence for believers. Read Acts 2:17.

Spontaneous Thoughts

Spontaneous "lights on" thoughts are when God gives you one of His thoughts. You learn to discern them with exercise. Spontaneous thoughts are a common, everyday occurrence for believers. Read Amos 4:13, Psalms 139:18, and 1 Corinthians 2:16.

Dreams

A dream is a vision while you sleep. Dreams are a common, everyday occurrence for believers. Read Acts 2:17.

HOW DOES GOD SPEAK?

Impressions and Knowings

An impression or knowing is when you automatically know something about somebody because the Spirit of God downloaded it to your spirit. Impressions and knowings are a common, everyday occurrence for believers. Read Matthew 9:4.

Bearing Another's Burdens Physically and Emotionally

It's when you feel a spiritual attack, or when you experience the emotional or physical pain that someone else is going through, and you pray for, walk with, understand, or help them overcome it. It's the deepest way to understand what someone else is going through. God often communicates words of knowledge and gives you discernment of spirits this way. What you are feeling might not be just you! It's a common, everyday occurrence for believers. Read Galatians 6:2.

Five Spiritual Senses: Taste, Feel, Smell, See, and Hear

In Hebrews 5:14, we are exhorted to mature through the constant exercise of our spiritual senses. As you learn and grow in walking in the Spirit, you learn to discern through your five spiritual senses. Above, we've already talked about feeling, seeing, and hearing with your spiritual senses; you can also taste and smell. Heaven often smells sweet and refreshing. Demonic operations usually have a foul and negative odor. In Ezekiel 3:3, after eating a spiritual scroll, he said that it tasted sweet like honey. Receiving a revelation from God through your five spiritual senses is a common, everyday occurrence for believers.

A Scripture Comes to Mind

It's when Jesus gives you a specific verse that meets someone right where they're at and communicates His love, victory, and edification. The Bible is our foundation and authority for everything we do! A scripture coming to mind is a common, everyday occurrence for believers. Read 2 Timothy 3:16-17.

God also speaks in many other ways, but those listed above are common for the everyday believer.

THREE-STEP PROCESS OF RECEIVING REVELATION FROM GOD

Receiving and applying revelation from Jesus can be summed up in the following three simple steps. Read them, memorize them, and apply them each time you receive a download from God. He's waiting to lead and direct you!

Revelation

First, you receive revelation from the Lord through a vision, His still, small voice, or you have a spontaneous thought, etc.

Interpretation

Next, you ask God for His interpretation of the revelation that was received. Remember, "It is the glory of God to conceal a matter; to search out a matter is the glory of kings" (Proverbs 25:2 NIV). He's waiting to interpret His revelation for you.

Application

Lastly, you inquire of God for His application of the revelation received. I probably only share twenty percent of what I see and hear in the Spirit. The rest is applied without communicating with others.

One of the most important prophetic lessons you can learn is that just because you see or hear it, that doesn't mean you say it!

CHAPTER 3
PROPHETIC GUIDELINES

Imagine a train with train tracks. The train represents the (*rhema*) prophetic spoken Word of God. The train tracks represent the (*logos*) written Word of God. Some churches have a lot of train tracks, but no train. Other churches have a lot of trains running around with no tracks, and people are getting hit, hurt, and wounded. For a thriving "Word of God centered" atmosphere, it's vital we have both! Below are some important train tracks as we learn to steward the train of the Holy Spirit's prophetic gifts.

Stay Within the Boundaries of Edification, Exhortation, and Comfort

The New Testament gift of prophecy is for encouragement, not discouragement. 1 Corinthians 14:3 says, "But he who prophesies speaks edification and exhortation and comfort to men." Ephesians 6:17 tells us that the spoken Word of God is a sword. As God gives you a word, it becomes a sword. You can either equip someone or stab someone with it. Aim to edify and build up!

Be Governed by Love

1 Corinthians 13:2 (NIV) says, "If I have the gift of prophecy and can fathom all mysteries and all knowledge, and if I have a faith that can move mountains, but do not have love, I am nothing." Make love your aim. In God's eyes, love is more important than gifting. Pursue love first, then desire spiritual gifts. When love is our aim, the prophetic flows easily.

Treasure Hunt

One of Satan's names is the accuser of the brethren (Revelation 12:9-11). He loves to get into prophetic circles and point out issues in the guise of discernment. It's a loveless trap! It's easy to find an issue. Look for the gold God placed inside someone. The prophetic hunts for treasure!

Communicate from a Spirit of Humility

Rather than yelling loudly, "The Lord sayeth unto thee …," communicate in a down-to-earth manner with people. Some suggestions on how to begin are "I sense …," "I feel like God is saying, …," or "Does this mean anything to you?" Allow the recipient to weigh the words for themselves. If you come across as controlling or "super spiritual," your word won't be received.

Don't Be Afraid to Fail

1 Corinthians 14:31 says, " For you can all prophesy one by one, that all may learn and all may be encouraged." In other words, no one learns without making mistakes. Learning to prophesy is no different than learning to teach, evangelize, or to play an instrument. Perfectionism is the biggest cork to learning to prophesy. Stay clothed with humility and

aim to learn from your mistakes. If you make a mess, clean it up. Practice makes progress.

Prophesy the Solution, Not the Problem

If you discern a problem, ask the Lord for His solution. This is called flip-flopping. Aim to edify.

The Goal Isn't to Correct and Rebuke People

Our aim is to edify, exhort, and comfort one another. Our goal is to love people with the reckless love of Jesus. Corrective words are reserved for those who operate in the governmental office of a prophet, and a corrective rebuke should come as a last resort, never a first response. We should never correct someone we haven't wept for, and a corrective word should be aimed at calling someone forward, not pushing them back.

Slowdown, Cowboy!

When learning to prophesy, refrain from prophesying about mates, dates, babies, or major relocations until you are fully developed in the prophetic gifts. Many lives have been wrecked by these types of words given loosely and immaturely. Does God prophesy these things? Yes, but considering the damage these types of words have done in lives, walk in the fear of the Lord and tread lightly. We will be accountable for what we prophesy.

Don't Despise Small Beginnings

In John 1:43-51, Jesus sees Nathanael sitting under a tree and hears simple encouragement for him, saying, "Here truly is an Israelite in whom there is no deceit." This word rocked Nathanael to the core. Simple love-loaded encouragement from the Lord is priceless. The prophetic gift is like a muscle; the more you use it, the more definition and detail you'll find. Be faithful in the long run. You'll grow in greater detail and definition when you prophesy!

Stick to the Bible. Revelatory words will never contradict Scripture. Let's get excited to prophesy!

speaks to you. Record what He says. You just received a love-loaded word from the creator of the universe!

Exercising Encouraging Others

The following three exercises are great activators for you to hear and see God's voice for others. Find people in your sphere to practice on, share with them by saying, "I'm learning how to hear God's voice for His specific encouragement, and I'd love to practice on you!" Knowing you are learning, most people feel like they are helping you out, and it makes it a little less awkward. Make sure to exercise with a smile on your face and keep your eyes open. Let's go!

- **One Word Exercise:** Ask Jesus for one encouraging word and wait until He speaks. As you wait, lean in and inquire about the person's specific gifts, talents, strengths, and character qualities. As you receive your one word, describe it to the person in a paragraph. For example, "I'm hearing the word 'courageous,' and I feel like God is showing me that you have a bold and courageous heart toward things others would be intimidated by. You are a strong and courageous leader." In John 1,

Jesus encouraged Nathanael by saying he was a man of no guile. This simple encouragement made a huge impact on Nathanael's life.

- **Animal Exercise:** Ask Jesus to show you an animal that illustrates a quality that this person has and wait until He speaks. He's relational and loves interacting with you on a personal level. As you receive your animal illustration, share with the person about the animal the Lord showed you and how it illustrates a quality in their life. For example, "I'm seeing a 'mountain lion,' and I feel like God is showing me that you are a mountain-conqueror and ferocious in warfare when it comes to dealing with the enemy." In Isaiah 40:31, God says we will mount up on wings like eagles, using an animal to illustrate and communicate His Word to His people. Animals are a common illustration biblically!

- **Cartoon Exercise:** Ask Jesus to show you a cartoon character that illustrates a quality that this person has and wait until He speaks. He's relational and loves interacting with you on a personal level. As you receive your cartoon illustration, share with the person about the cartoon the Lord showed you and how it illustrates a quality in their life. For example, "I'm seeing Batman, and I feel like God is showing me that you have a strong heartbeat for justice and making wrong things right. You like to protect the underdog, and there's safety in your stead." Just as Jesus uses animals to illustrate a word, He can also use cartoons!

Exercise brings strength and definition. Like going to a gym, these exercises will work out your prophetic muscles and make them stronger and more defined. Do you desire more detail in your hearing? Do you desire to operate in a stronger prophetic anointing? Exercise! The Lord rewards the faithful. The greatest key to growing in the prophetic is intimacy with Jesus! Practice daily.

CHAPTER 5
TESTING THE VOICE

As you grow in hearing God's voice, you'll learn to discern the difference between the voice of God, yourself, and the enemy. It says in 1 Thessalonians 5:19-21, "Do not quench the Spirit. Do not despise prophecies. Test all things; hold fast what is good."

It's vital that we test what we deliver and what we receive to avoid a counterfeit spirit. Jesus assures us with confidence in John 10:4-5, when He says, "… the sheep follow him, for they know his voice. Yet they will by no means follow a stranger, but will flee from him, for they do not know the voice of strangers." As you grow in discerning and learning the voice of God, you'll catch the enemy's voice quicker and more precise. Exercise is your key!

SEVEN KEYS TO HELP TEST THE VOICE YOU'RE HEARING

1. God's Voice Will Always Line Up with Scripture

Acts 17:11 says, "These were more fair-minded than those in Thessalonica, in that they received the word with all readiness, and searched the Scriptures daily to find out whether these things were so."

2. God's Voice Will Always Line Up with His Character and Nature Seen In Scripture

Loving, powerful, patient, Prince of Peace, etc.

3. God's Voice Will Bear the Fruit of the Holy Spirit

Galatians 5:22-23 says, "But the fruit of the Spirit is love, joy, peace, longsuffering, kindness, goodness, faithfulness, gentleness, self-control …"

4. God's Voice Will Bear Witness in Your Spirit, with His Spirit Inside of You

You'll feel a "yes" in your heart! Romans 8:16 says, "The Spirit Himself bears witness with our spirit that we are children of God."

5. God's Spoken Word Will Carry a Residue of Glory as You Review and Rehearse It

Hebrews 4:12 says, "For the word of God is living and powerful, …"

6. God Will Confirm His Word with Two or Three Witnesses to Establish It in Your Heart

Ask Him for confirmation! 2 Corinthians 13:1 says, "…By the mouth of two or three witnesses every word shall be established."

7. The Voice of the Flesh and the Voice of the Enemy Can Sound the Same

They are both very selfish. Jesus spoke to Satan, speaking through Peter, "Get behind Me, Satan! You are an offense to Me, for you are not mindful of the things of God, but the things of men"

> (Matthew 16:23). Galatians 5:19-21 says, "Now the works of the flesh are evident, which are: adultery, fornication, uncleanness, lewdness, idolatry, sorcery, hatred, contentions, jealousies, outbursts of wrath, selfish ambitions, dissensions, heresies, envy, murders, drunkenness, revelries, and the like; …"

If you hear a voice that doesn't line up with the seven keys, command it to be quiet in the name of Jesus. If someone gives you a "prophetic" word and it doesn't align with the seven keys, don't fear. Simply smile and say, "Thank you. I'll bring this to the Lord." And when you are alone, break agreement with and declare those words powerless.

If you feel like you are hearing God's voice but aren't sure, simply put the word on the shelf and ask Jesus for confirmation. Understanding these keys can be helpful, but remember, give yourself and others grace to learn, grow, and make mistakes. You are God's kid, and you are worthy, righteous, and forgiven, especially when you make a mistake. Mistakes and growing pains come with the territory of growing in the prophetic.

CHAPTER 6
STEWARD YOUR WORD

Recognize that prophetic words are not automatic, and they aren't guaranteed. Seeing God's promise fulfilled in your life requires: obedient partnership, understanding the timing, and warfare. In Numbers 13, twelve spies had the prophetic promise from God, but only two of them, Joshua and Caleb, held fast to the promise and saw it come to pass. Personal prophetic words are conditional because each of us has free will. The following are some steps to steward your word:

Test It

As shared in depth above, never assume a word is from the Lord. Test it (1 Thessalonians 5:20-21). Does it bear witness and resonate in your spirit with the Holy Spirit (Romans 8:16)? Does it align with God's written Word? Is it in line with the Lord's character and nature (Galatians 5:22-23)? Does it confirm a word that the Lord has already spoken to you (2 Corinthians 13:1)? If it doesn't align with God's Word or character, shake it off. If you're unsure whether it resonates with or bears witness to your spirit, put it on the shelf and ask the Lord for confirmation.

Get Specifics

Ask the Lord for specifics regarding the word given to avoid misunderstanding and disappointment. Be careful not to assume! In Judges 6:12 (NIV), the angel of the Lord prophesied to Gideon, saying, "The LORD is with you, mighty warrior." But after Gideon received his word, he inquired of the Lord and received specific details about what his word meant. In Jeremiah 1, Jeremiah dialogued with the Lord and received greater detail of his prophetic word.

Timing

Ask the Lord for His timing to avoid trying to make your word happen before it's time and to avoid missing your word's fulfillment by holding back when it is time to step forward. Genesis 15-20 recounts God's prophetic word to Abraham for a son and how Abraham tried to make his word happen before its time by sleeping with his slave, Hagar. She birthed Ishmael—a clear picture of trying to make the word you were given happen in your own strength. Wait in faith for God's timing! God was merciful to Abraham and still brought His word to pass through Abraham's wife, Sarah, who conceived and gave birth to Isaac.

Partnership

Ask the Lord for His clear steps to partner with Him to see His word fulfilled in your life. In Judges 6 and 7, after Gideon received the specifics of his prophetic word, the Lord gave him steps to partner with Him to see the word fulfilled. Partnership is vital to seeing your word fulfilled!

Warfare

Paul exhorts you to wage the good warfare regarding the prophetic words spoken over your life (1 Timothy 1:18-19). The enemy aims to steal, kill, and destroy (John 10:10). Therefore, put on the whole armor of God and protect what God has spoken over your life (Ephesians 6:12-18). Write down your prophetic words and confess them often! Greater words require greater warfare, but God's authority rests on you to see the enemy defeated and His Word come to pass in your life!

CHAPTER 7
PROPHETIC EVANGELISM

What is prophetic evangelism? Is it biblical? In the following verses, Jesus demonstrates the basics of hearing the Father's specific word for an unbeliever, delivering it in love, and the impact that awaits. 1 Corinthians 14:24-25 lays out the power and impact that prophetic evangelism has on lives. Look it up!

In John 4, Jesus demonstrates prophetic evangelism with the woman at the well. May it stir us up to do the same. Let's bring the harvest in with prophetic power!

Next, we are going to read through John 1:45-51, step-by-step, and see Jesus in action.

Nathanael is told about Jesus and is skeptical.

"Philip found Nathanael and said to him, 'We have found Him of whom Moses in the law, and also the prophets, wrote—Jesus of Nazareth, the son of Joseph.' And Nathanael said to him, 'Can anything good come out of Nazareth?'"

Nathanael is encouraged by a believer.

"Philip said to him, 'Come and see.'"

Jesus releases a simple prophetic word of knowledge, highlighting the nationality and character of Nathanael—love-loaded!

"Jesus saw Nathanael coming toward Him, and said of him, 'Behold, an Israelite indeed, in whom is no deceit!'"

The anointing, love, and accuracy of the simple word spoken are felt by and stuns Nathanael.

*"Nathanael said to Him,
'How do You know me?'"*

Jesus tuned into the Holy Spirit when he saw Nathanael sitting under a fig tree. Prophetic evangelism 101!

*"Jesus answered and said to him,
'Before Philip called you, when you were under the fig tree, I saw you.'"*

The love-loaded prophetic word from Jesus opened Nathanael's eyes, causing him to believe in Jesus!

*"Nathanael answered and said to Him,
'Rabbi, You are the Son of God!
You are the King of Israel!'"*

> Discipleship begins.
>
> *"Jesus answered and said to him, 'Because I said to you, "I saw you under the fig tree," do you believe? You will see greater things than these.' And He said to him, 'Most assuredly, I say to you, hereafter you shall see heaven open, and the angels of God ascending and descending upon the Son of Man.'"*

In summary:

1. Tune into the Holy Spirit when you see someone.
2. Deliver what you see and hear as the Holy Spirit leads—love-loaded!
3. You'll see simple words from Jesus open up eyes to who He is.
4. After the impact and leading to Jesus, build a relationship. It's discipleship time.

CHAPTER 8
ALIGNED WITH OIL

Authorized only, please! Did you know that you only have authority where you are under authority? This was a painful lesson for me to learn. When I first came to Christ, I was very zealous, but very independent and self-righteous. I had no idea how authority worked in the kingdom. As prophetic believers, it's a vital truth to understand.

Psalm 133:1-3 (NIV) says, "How good and pleasant it is when God's people live together in unity! It is like precious oil poured on the head, running down on the beard, running down on Aaron's beard, down on the collar of his robe. It is as if the dew of Hermon were falling on Mount Zion. For there the LORD bestows his blessing, even life forevermore."

In God's kingdom, the oil flows from the head down. In the full chapter of Psalm 133, we see that the oil flows from the head down, as described biblically. Oil symbolizes the moving and operation of the Holy Spirit. The head represents authority.

As prophetic voices, we must come under God's established authority in order to have authority. Think of it like this: the oil comes down through authority, and as you honor those in authority in your life, you come into alignment with the oil of the Holy Spirit that flows from the head down.

Having a submissive heart toward authority is one of the most valuable character qualities a believer can possess. Remember, no authority exists except the authority God has established in your life (Romans 13:1-2). This pertains to governmental authority, authority in the home and business arena, and spiritual authority in the church.

As you trust God's sovereign hand working through those in authority in your life (Proverbs 21:1), you'll find where you are authorized to prophesy. Trust Him to make a way! Books could be written on this subject, but here's the main point: keep honor of authority your priority as you blossom in the prophetic gifts of the Holy Spirit. The book *Under Cover*[6] by John Bevere does a great job of hitting this subject home—a highly recommended read!

CONCLUSION
LEARN IT, OWN IT, MULTIPLY!

This packet aims to provide believers with a concise and clear understanding of the basics and guidelines for operating in the prophetic gifts, along with activations and exercises to put them into practice.

Remember this: the prophetic is like a muscle, so the more you use it, the more definition and strength you'll experience in it. Exercise and practice often! Use the above material as a resource to learn to test your words and steward the words you receive from others.

And lastly, in 2 Timothy 2:2 (NAS), Paul exhorts us, saying, "The things which you have heard from me in the presence of many witnesses, entrust these to faithful people who will be able to teach others also."

In other words, as you learn and own the joy of operating and functioning in the prophetic gifts of the Holy Spirit, train and teach others to do the same. Before every other spiritual gift, Paul exhorts us to especially desire to prophesy (1 Corinthians 14:1). God is raising up a prophetic remnant in these last days who know His voice and make Him known on the earth. Please feel free to use this book to equip, train, activate, and launch others to do the same.

Kawika Cornelius

Freedom and Joy Ministries, Loveland, Colorado

ABOUT THE AUTHOR

Kawika Cornelius is a revivalist with a passion for raising up revivalists. With a heart to equip believers in the finished work of the cross, the character and call of Spirit-filled leadership, powerful evangelism, and a supernatural lifestyle, he has trained and activated thousands to walk boldly in their faith. As a prophetic voice, Kawika carries a mandate to take the gospel beyond the four walls of the church, teaching believers to hear God clearly for themselves and others.

His journey with Jesus began in 1998, when he encountered the Lord and was baptized in the Holy

Spirit while in the county jail, facing prison time. That moment ignited a fire that has never gone out. In 2002, while completing his second year of ministry training in the Master's Commission, a devastating car accident left him paralyzed from the chest down. Refusing to let tragedy silence his call, Kawika went on to earn both his associate's and bachelor's in theology from Beacon University: Institute of Ministry Training.

In 2011, he planted Freedom and Joy Christian Center in Northern Colorado, a hub for encountering and equipping, where he continues to serve as senior leader. His ministry has also reached jails, nursing homes, and the nations, marked by prophetic accuracy, healings, miracles, outbreaks of joy, and tangible demonstrations of the Holy Spirit. While contending for his own healing, Kawika burns to see lives transformed and bodies restored by the power of Jesus.

CONNECT WITH KAWIKA

www.freedomandjoycc.org
YouTube: Kawika Cornelius
TikTok: KawikaTokTik

ENDNOTES

1 "Strong's #5042 – עָבַן – Old Testament Hebrew Lexical Dictionary." *StudyLight.Org*, www.studylight.org/lexicons/eng/hebrew/5042.html.

2 *Strong's Hebrew: 5030. אִיבָן (Nabi) – Prophet, Prophets, Prophecy*, biblehub.com/hebrew/5030.htm.

3 *Strong's Greek: 4395. Προφητεύω (Prophéteuó) – to Prophesy, to Speak Forth by Divine Inspiration, to Predict*, biblehub.com/greek/4395.htm.

4 Ibid.

5 Randolph, Larry. *User Friendly Prophecy: Guidelines for the Effective Use of Prophecy*. Destiny Image, Inc, 1998.

6 Bevere, John, and Tom Parks. *Under Cover: Why Your Response to Leadership Determines Your Future*. Thomas Nelson Publishers, 2018.

Made in the USA
Coppell, TX
22 January 2026

69116608R00036